Piano Grades 1–2

Pam Wedgwood

Contents *page*

1.	Moanin'	Timmons	*2*
2.	Tik-tak	Wedgwood	*3*
3.	I wan'na be like you (the monkey song)	Sherman & Sherman	*4*
4.	Thinking of you	Wedgwood	*6*
5.	Some day my prince will come	Morey & Churchill	*8*
6.	All sold out	Wedgwood	*10*
7.	Blue Monk	Monk	*11*
8.	Summertime	Gershwin, Gershwin, Heyward & Heyward	*12*
9.	Don't blame me!	Wedgwood	*14*
10.	Let's jazz	Wedgwood	*15*
11.	Nice work if you can get it	Gershwin & Gershwin	*16*
12.	In the mood	Garland & Razaf	*18*
13.	Let's call the whole thing off	Gershwin & Gershwin	*20*
14.	Lullaby of Birdland	Shearing & Weiss	*22*
15.	Love is here to stay	Gershwin & Gershwin	*24*

First published in 2006 by Faber Music Ltd
Bloomsbury House 74–77 Great Russell Street London WC1B 3DA
Cover design by Stik
Music processed by MusicSet 2000
Printed in England by Caligraving Ltd

ISBN10: 0-571-52477-X
EAN13: 978-0-571-52477-8

To buy Faber Music publications or to find out about the full range of titles available please contact your local music retailer or Faber Music sales enquiries:

Faber Music Limited, Burnt Mill, Elizabeth Way, Harlow CM20 2HX
Tel: +44 (0)1279 82 89 82 Fax: +44 (0)1279 82 89 83
sales@fabermusic.com fabermusic.com

1. Moanin'

Words and music by Robert Timmons
arr. Wedgwood

2. Tik-tak

Pam Wedgwood

3. I wan'na be like you (the monkey song)

Words and music by Richard M. Sherman and Robert B. Sherman
arr. Wedgwood

a tempo
poco rit.
a tempo
1.
2.

4. Thinking of you

Pam Wedgwood

21
25
mp
30
mf
f
34
38
dim.
pp

5. Some day my prince will come

Words and music by Larry Morey and Frank Churchill
arr. Wedgwood

26
mp
31
poco rit.
a tempo
f
mf
36
poco rit.
mp
41
a tempo
mf
46
p

6. All sold out

*grace notes optional

7. Blue Monk

Groovy ♩ = 112
Music by Thelonious Monk
arr. Wedgwood
rit.
D.C. to ⊕ then to Coda
CODA

8. Summertime

Words and music by George Gershwin, Ira Gershwin, DuBose Heyward and Dorothy Heyward
arr. Wedgwood

Lazily, with a gentle swing ♩ = 72

p mp

5

9

mp

13

mf

17

mp p mf

21
25
mp
29
33
mp
p
37
poco rit.
pp

9. Don't blame me!

Pam Wedgwood

10. Let's jazz

Pam Wedgwood

11. Nice work if you can get it

Words and music by George and Ira Gershwin
arr. Wedgwood

Smooth, gentle swing ♩ = 92

25
mp
3
29
f
33
mf
37
41
poco rit.
f
p

12. In the mood

Words by Andy Razaf
Music by Joe Garland
arr. Wedgwood

21
mf
1 2 3
24
mf
1.
2.
27
f
f
31
mp
5 4
35
39
f

13. Let's call the whole thing off

Words and music by George and Ira Gershwin
arr. Wedgwood

16
f
19
mf
23
27
f
poco rit.
mf
30
a tempo
f
p
Ped.

14. Lullaby of Birdland

Words by George David Weiss
Music by George Shearing
arr. Wedgwood

shout
two three four

15. Love is here to stay